I0165163

MINDFULNESS
is
THE WAY:

A JOURNEY TO PRESENCE,
PEACE, AND PURPOSE

MINDFULNESS
is
THE WAY:

A JOURNEY TO PRESENCE,
PEACE, AND PURPOSE

**CHRISTIAN MINDFULNESS
GOD'S WAY**

RYAN C. NEAL, MD

ABOVE CONSCIOUSNESS PUBLISHING
ISBN: 979-8-9912763-3-7

All scripture quotes and references are taken from the public domain unless otherwise specified.
'Mindfulness is The Way: *A Journey to Presence, Peace, and Purpose*'
© 2025 Ryan C. Neal, MD

Copyright notice: All rights reserved under the International and Pan-American Copyright Conventions. No part of this book may be reproduced or transmitted in any form or by any means, electronic or mechanical, including photocopying, recording, or by any information storage and retrieval system, without permission in writing from the publisher.

Warning: the unauthorized reproduction or distribution of this copyrighted work is illegal. Criminal copyright infringement, including infringement without monetary gain, is investigated by the FBI and is punishable by up to 5 years in prison and a fine of $250,000.

This book is dedicated to my late mother 'Nana' and to all her children, grandchildren, and great- grandchildren.

TABLE OF CONTENTS

CHAPTER REVIEW

Chapter 1: The Wake-Up Call
A modern life demands a mindful shift.

Modern chaos and constant noise have numbed us to our own divine presence. Living on autopilot, we disconnect from ourselves, others, and God. But the soul longs to awaken. Through a deeply personal story, the author shares how one quiet moment became the catalyst for change, an invitation to walk the sacred path of mindfulness—not as a trend, but as a spiritual return to what matters most.

Chapter 2: What Is Mindfulness, Really?
Beyond buzzwords into embodied truth.

Mindfulness is not stress relief; it is sacred awareness. With roots in ancient spiritual traditions and validation from modern neuroscience, mindfulness is both practice and presence. Differentiated from meditation, it is a way of being, anchored in the present moment where transformation unfolds. This chapter reclaims mindfulness as a divine practice for living awake and aligned.

Chapter 3: The Mindful Mind
From mental noise to mental clarity.

The mind is a narrator—but not always a truthful one. Mindfulness reveals the space between our thoughts and our identity. Through spiritual insight and reflective exercises, the reader learns to witness thoughts without judgment, replacing reactivity with divine clarity. This chapter is a masterclass in compassionate mental awareness.

Chapter 4: The Breath as Your Anchor

Your inhale is your invitation home.

Breath is not just a biological function—it is Spirit's rhythm within us. In this chapter, the reader explores breath as a portal to presence and healing. Techniques such as 4-7-8 and box breathing become holy tools for nervous system regulation, grounding, and deepening connection with God.

Chapter 5: The Body Remembers

The body keeps score—but it also holds wisdom.

Mindfulness moves from the mind into the body. By learning to listen to tension, sensation, and intuition, the reader is invited to experience the body as a sacred vessel. Through somatic practices like the body scan and mindful walking, healing and integration unfold.

Chapter 6: Emotional Alchemy

Feel it, to free it.

Emotions are not problems to fix but messages to receive. In this tender chapter, the reader learns how to hold space for grief, fear, and anger with compassion. Mindfulness becomes the ground for emotional healing, transforming pain into presence and suffering into sacred insight.

Chapter 7: The Sacred Now

God meets you in the moment.

All of life unfolds in the present moment. This chapter explores how God, as the great I AM, dwells not in our regrets or projections, but in the holy immediacy of now. Through awe, gratitude, and stillness, the reader is called into the sacred sanctuary of the present.

Chapter 8: Mindful Relationships
Presence is the language of love.

Mindfulness deepens love. Through spiritual presence and compassionate communication, the reader learns how to stay grounded in relationships, especially during conflict or challenge. Practices of deep listening, boundaries, and grace transform connection into communion.

Chapter 9: The Noise Detox
Silence is not empty, it's full of answers.

In a world addicted to distraction, silence becomes salvation. The reader is guided to reclaim sacred quiet through digital sabbaths, intentional stillness, and spiritual fasting from overstimulation. Here, silence is reframed not as emptiness but as the fullness of divine presence.

Chapter 10: Purpose, Flow, and the Present Path
You are most powerful when you are present.

Purpose is not something to chase—it's something to align with. Through flow states, harmony over hustle, and daily rituals of sacred intention, the reader learns to walk their calling mindfully. Each breath becomes a step in the divine rhythm of their becoming.

Chapter 11: Mindfulness in Suffering
Even in darkness, the Way remains.

Pain does not negate the presence of God. This chapter walks with the reader through grief, trauma, and uncertainty, showing how mindfulness becomes a companion through the valley. Through surrender, trust, and compassionate presence, suffering becomes sacred space.

Chapter 12: Becoming the Way

Your life becomes your message.

Mindfulness is no longer a practice—it is a way of being. This final chapter calls the reader to embody presence as their life's posture, their soul's offering. Through daily rituals, aligned living, and a 30-day mindfulness roadmap, the journey becomes a lifestyle. The reader becomes the walking sanctuary, the Way itself.

Epilogue: The Journey Continues

This is not the end. It is a new beginning. Every breath, every moment, every now is an invitation to return to the sacred, to live awake, and to walk in peace. Mindfulness is not a destination. It is the Way. And now, it is yours to live.

CHAPTER 1:

THE WAKE-UP CALL

*A modern life demands
a mindful shift.*

The Modern Chaos and Constant Noise

> We live in a world that never stops talking.

From the moment we wake up, we are surrounded by a symphony of distractions. Notifications buzz before the sun even rises. News feeds clamor for our outrage. Advertisements whisper that we are not enough. Schedules fill with obligations. We run from one commitment to the next, often forgetting what we were even rushing toward in the first place.

Modern life, for all its innovation and connectivity, is increasingly becoming a life of disconnection. Not from technology—but from the self.

This relentless outer noise has become the soundtrack of our lives, drowning out the subtle whispers of our inner voice. The voice of intuition. The voice of peace. The voice of God.

We are "connected" 24/7, and yet many of us have never felt more isolated, more scattered, more unsure of who we are or what we're really doing here.

Something has to change.

And that change begins with waking up.

Why We're Living on Autopilot

Most of us don't consciously choose chaos. We don't decide to become anxious, hurried, numb, or irritable. It happens slowly—over time. Like fog rolling in. We find ourselves performing our lives rather than living them.

The truth is, we've been programmed—by culture, by trauma, by systems—to value doing over being. Success over stillness. Productivity over presence.

We wake up. We check our phones. We drink our coffee. We rush. We work. We respond. We scroll. We react. We numb. We repeat.

Autopilot isn't just a habit. It's a coping mechanism. A survival strategy. But the cost of this unconscious living is steep: we lose our vitality, our clarity, and our ability to hear God's voice within.

> We become strangers to ourselves.
>
> Mindfulness is the way home.

The Pain of Disconnection

There is a deep ache that lives quietly inside so many of us. An unnamable restlessness. A hunger. A longing to feel more alive, more connected, more grounded, more whole.

We search for it in relationships. In jobs. In self-help books. In social media likes. In spiritual performance.

But none of it sticks. Because what we are actually craving is presence. Connection. Communion. And not just with others—but with ourselves and the Divine.

The greatest illusion of our time is the belief that we are separate— from each other, from creation, and from God. And that illusion breeds fear, anxiety, insecurity, competition, and despair.

But when we pause... when we breathe... when we notice... we begin to remember the truth:

We were never meant to live this way.
We were never meant to live so far from ourselves.
We were created for awareness. For embodiment. For Spirit-filled presence.

Mindfulness is not a wellness trend. It is a return to that which is most sacred: *being here.*

A Personal Story of Realization

My own wake-up call didn't arrive with a crash. It came in a whisper.

It came after years of striving. Years of high achievement, of performance, of doing all the right things. My calendar was full, my inbox overflowing, my reputation strong. But my soul was silent. I couldn't feel myself anymore. I had lost touch with the part of me that simply *was*—not the part that achieved, not the part that planned, but the part that listened, the part that knew.

One day, in the midst of yet another busy morning, I stopped. Not because I wanted to—but because I had to. My body wouldn't let me go on. I sat still in my chair and heard nothing but the sound of my breath.

It was in that moment of stillness that something shifted. I felt the presence of God—not in the sky, but within me. Not in a sermon, but in the silence.

That moment changed everything. It was as if I'd taken off a blindfold I didn't know I was wearing.

From that day forward, I began a journey—not to escape my life, but to live it more fully. More mindfully.

Invitation to Walk The Way of Mindfulness

This book is not just a collection of teachings—it is an invitation. A sacred calling back to the present moment. Back to your body. Back to your soul. Back to God.

Mindfulness is The Way because mindfulness is the pathway back to what matters most.

It is the sacred art of becoming awake in your own life. It is learning how to pause in the storm, how to find stillness in the noise, how to feel without fear, and how to love without needing to control.

This is a journey inward—but also upward. A path that blends mindfulness with faith. Presence with purpose. Stillness with Spirit.

And it begins here.

Right now.

With a breath.

Breathe.
You're here.
You're home.
Let's begin.

CHAPTER 2:

WHAT IS MINDFULNESS, REALLY?

Beyond buzzwords into embodied truth.

Definitions and Misconceptions

We hear the word everywhere—on wellness podcasts, in therapy rooms, on meditation apps, even in corporate board meetings.

"Be mindful."
"Practice mindfulness."
"Try mindfulness for stress."

But what does mindfulness *actually* mean?

Many people equate mindfulness with relaxation or a method for stress reduction. While it *can* produce calm and emotional balance, mindfulness is not about escaping discomfort or numbing emotion. It's not a shortcut to inner peace or a way to avoid life's complexity.

Mindfulness is a quality of being.

It is the ability to be fully awake to what is happening *right now*, without judgment and without resistance.

Mindfulness is sacred awareness. It is remembering that you are alive—and that this moment, just as it is, is holy ground.

It is not a quick fix.
It is not a passive state.
It is not self-help dressed in yoga pants.

Mindfulness is a powerful return—to presence, to truth, to Spirit.

It is not about *changing* your life. It's about *showing up* for the one you already have.

Eastern Roots and Western Science

Mindfulness is not new. It is ancient.

Its roots trace back thousands of years to the teachings of the Buddha, where the Pali word *sati* was used to describe a type of awareness that involves remembering—remembering to return to the present, to the breath, to the truth of impermanence and inner peace.

In Eastern traditions, mindfulness is deeply woven into spiritual practice. It's the path to enlightenment, liberation, and union with the divine.

But over the past few decades, Western science has begun to validate what mystics and monks have known for centuries.

Neuroscience now shows that mindfulness changes the structure of the brain. It strengthens the prefrontal cortex—the part of the brain responsible for decision-making and focus—while shrinking the amygdala, which governs fear and reactivity.

Psychology confirms that mindfulness improves emotional regulation, increases compassion, and reduces anxiety, depression, and even chronic pain.

Even corporate leaders are embracing mindfulness—not just for productivity, but for clarity, creativity, and connection.

What was once a sacred spiritual path is now a scientifically supported practice for well-being. But in truth, it has *always* been both.

Mindfulness is where the sacred and the scientific meet.
It's not *either/or*—it's *yes/and*.
A timeless practice for a modern soul.

Mindfulness vs. Meditation

Many people think mindfulness and meditation are the same thing. But that's only partially true.

Meditation is a formal practice—something you *do*. You might sit in silence, follow your breath, repeat a mantra, or visualize light. It often happens in a specific place, for a specific time.

Mindfulness is a way of being—something you *live*. It is the continuous practice of presence in everyday life. Washing dishes. Driving to work. Listening to your partner. Savoring a bite of food. Feeling your feet touch the earth.

Meditation can help train your mind to be more mindful. But you don't need to sit on a cushion for 30 minutes a day to live a mindful life.

You can live mindfully in the classroom.
You can live mindfully at the bedside.
You can live mindfully as a parent, a CEO, a cashier, or a pastor.
You don't need incense.
You don't need silence.
You just need *attention*—and *intention*.

> Meditation may open the door.
> Mindfulness is how you walk through it.

The Sacred Power of "Now"

Presence is the portal to peace.

So much of our suffering stems from living *anywhere* but here. We replay the past. We rehearse the future. We resist what's happening. We chase what's not.

But the truth is this: **life only ever happens in the present moment.**

God speaks *now*.
Healing happens *now*.
Love lives *now*.

The present moment is not just a psychological state—it is a spiritual one. The "now" is where the ego dissolves and the soul awakens. It's where we stop performing and start being. It's where we meet ourselves—and where we meet God.

Mindfulness trains us to return to the now, over and over again. Not to escape life, but to *enter it fully*.

Every breath is a chance to begin again.
Every moment is a new altar.
Every "now" is an invitation to the sacred.

The Presence That Transforms
Presence isn't passive—it's powerful. It changes everything.

When you become mindful, you begin to see yourself clearly. You notice your patterns. You catch your reactions. You interrupt your habits. You hold space for your emotions.

You stop being *run by* your life, and you start *responding to* it—with wisdom, grace, and compassion.

Mindfulness teaches you how to be the witness and not the whirlpool.
How to feel without drowning.
How to speak without wounding.
How to live without leaving yourself behind.

In your relationships, presence creates safety.
In your body, presence brings healing.
In your spirit, presence awakens divinity.

> Mindfulness is not about becoming someone new.
> It's about coming home to who you've always been—whole,
> worthy, and awake.

A Pause Before We Go On...
Before we move forward into the deeper practices, let's pause here.

Breathe in.
Breathe out.
Notice this moment.
This breath.
This awareness.

You are not behind.
You are not broken.
You are not lost.

You are here.
And *here* is where transformation begins.

Welcome to mindfulness—not as a concept, but as a way.
Not as information, but as a sacred invitation.
Not just to calm your life—but to come alive.

CHAPTER 3:

THE MINDFUL MIND

From mental noise to
mental clarity.

There is a hidden world within each of us. A world made not of stone or skin—but of thought.

It's where we interpret life. Where we create meaning. Where we tell ourselves stories about who we are, what the world is like, and what is or is not possible.

This world—this inner mind—can either be our sanctuary or our prison. A place of divine dialogue, or a space of relentless noise.

For most of us, it has become the latter.

The Invisible Conversation
I remember the day I first truly *heard* my thoughts.

It wasn't that they weren't there before—they were always there. But I had never *noticed* them as something *separate* from me. I had never questioned them. I had never paused long enough to ask:

Whose voice is that?
Who is talking to me... about me?

It happened in a quiet moment—one of those rare, sacred silences where you're not doing anything but simply being.

In that stillness, I heard a voice in my mind say, *"You're not doing enough."*

At first, I reacted the way I always had—tense up, make a to-do list, fill the silence with effort. But something inside whispered back:

Is that the voice of truth... or the voice of fear?

That question changed everything. It was the beginning of my journey into what I now call *The Mindful Mind*—the space between stimulus and response, between thought and truth, between reaction and revelation.

Understanding Thoughts Without Being Trapped by Them
Most people live as if their thoughts are facts.

We think it, and so we believe it.
We assume that if our mind says something, it must be right.
But here's the truth: **your thoughts are not the voice of God.**
They are not even necessarily *your* voice.

Thoughts are habits.
Thoughts are echoes of the past.
Thoughts are the mind's way of predicting, protecting, and performing.

Some thoughts are wise. Some are neutral. Many are fearful, anxious, or repetitive. They are like clouds drifting across the sky. You can see them. You can name them. But you do not have to chase them.

The problem is not that we have thoughts. The problem is that we believe them without question.

But mindfulness invites a new way: **to witness your thoughts without being ruled by them.**

To realize: *I am not my thoughts. I am the one who notices them.*

Cultivating Awareness of Mental Chatter

The mind is a narrator—and it never runs out of things to say.

It comments on your appearance, your productivity, your relationships, your faith, your future. It replays conversations from five years ago and projects fears five years ahead.

Some of this chatter is rooted in love—your mind trying to protect you, warn you, prepare you. But much of it is rooted in fear, control, shame, and ego.

You're not enough.
What if you mess this up?
They didn't text back—what did you do wrong?
You should be farther along by now.
No one really understands you.

These are not spiritual truths. They are echoes of conditioning. Often, they are the voices of parents, teachers, cultures, or past traumas—not the voice of your soul, and certainly not the voice of God.

> God speaks in stillness.
> Fear speaks in noise.

The more we become aware of the chatter, the more space we create between ourselves and it. That space is called freedom.

Mindfulness teaches us to shift from *identification* to *observation*. From being *in* the thought to being *with* the thought. From being caught in the storm to watching it pass by from within the shelter of God's presence.

The Power of Observation Over Reaction

There is a sacred moment between thought and action. A holy pause between emotion and expression.

That space—that pause—is where freedom lives.
That space is where transformation happens.
That space is where God can speak.

This is the gift of metacognition: the ability to *think about your thinking*.

To observe the content of your mind with compassion and curiosity.

Not to shame it. Not to suppress it. But to gently say, *"I see you."*

When we develop this witnessing awareness, we interrupt the autopilot reactions that dominate so much of our life. We no longer explode in anger, spiral in anxiety, or collapse in shame. Instead, we respond. Consciously. Kindly. With wisdom.

This is not about becoming robotic. It's about becoming *free*.

Free to choose how you show up.
Free to speak with intention.
Free to move from Spirit, not fear.

Mindfulness is not about controlling your thoughts—it's about no longer letting them control *you*.

The Divine Witness Within

As I deepened my mindfulness practice, I began to sense something else in that space of awareness. Not just *my* consciousness—but *God's* presence.

I began to realize: the witness within me is also the witness *of* me.

The part of me that can observe my thoughts without judgment... is the part that is connected to the Divine.

> "Be still, and know that I am God."
> —Psalm 46:10

That scripture, for me, became a sacred map. Stillness is not the absence of thought—it is the awareness that thoughts are not God. It is the knowing that in stillness, we can hear something deeper.

Mindfulness is not merely psychological. It is spiritual. It is how we return to the Garden. How we walk with God in the cool of the day. How we remember that we are not our thoughts—we are God's beloved.

When we cultivate the mindful mind, we are not just training our brain. We are tuning our soul.

Exercises for Cognitive Clarity

1. Name the Voice
Take a moment to notice the thoughts running through your mind. Write down a few. Then ask:

- *Whose voice is this?*
- *Is this truth, fear, or conditioning?*
- *Would God speak to me this way?*

You'll be amazed how quickly the fog clears when you name the source of the noise.

2. Label the Thought

This practice helps to create space between you and the thought.

- *"That's a planning thought."*
- *"That's a fear story."*
- *"That's judgment."*
- *"That's a memory replay."*

Labeling reminds you: "I am the witness, not the thought."

3. The Sacred Pause

When you feel overwhelmed, pause for 10 seconds.

- Feel your breath.
- Place your hand on your heart.
- Say, *"God is here. I am here."*

This interrupts the reactivity spiral and opens the door to divine wisdom.

4. Mindfulness of Thinking Meditation

Sit quietly for 5 minutes.

- Focus on the breath.
- When a thought arises, notice it.
- Don't push it away. Just observe it, label it gently, and return to the breath.

This simple practice rewires the brain for clarity, compassion, and calm.

5. Scripture Reflection for Mental Renewal

Choose a verse that reminds you of your identity and God's presence. For example:

- *"You will keep in perfect peace all who trust in you, all whose thoughts are fixed on you."* —Isaiah 26:3

Write it down. Meditate on it. Let it become louder than your inner critic.

Closing Reflection: A New Way to Think
The mind is a beautiful servant but a terrible master.

When you live from unconscious thought, you live in bondage. But when you awaken to awareness, you live in peace.

Mindfulness doesn't erase your thoughts. It illumines them.

It helps you see the fear and invite in love.
It helps you notice the judgment and return to grace.
It helps you watch the clouds—and remember the sky.

You are not your thoughts.
You are the space between them.
You are the presence that observes.
You are the beloved of God, awake in your own soul.

Let the mind be a gateway, not a gatekeeper.
Let presence be your path.
Let mindfulness be your way.

Breathe.
Watch.
Witness.
Be.

This is the Mindful Mind.
This is freedom.
This is The Way.

CHAPTER 4:

THE BREATH AS YOUR ANCHOR

Your inhale is your invitation home.

> "Then the Lord God formed the man from the dust of the ground.
> He breathed the breath of life into the man's nostrils,
> and the man became a living being."
> —Genesis 2:7

There is a moment in every life when all we can do is breathe.

We reach the end of our understanding, the edge of our strength, the cliff of our capacity—and in that sacred pause, the only thing left is breath. No words. No plan. No performance. Just the gentle rhythm of inhale and exhale.

I have come to believe that in those moments, we are closer to God than we realize.

Because breath is not just biology—it is sacred.

It was the first gift given to humanity in the Garden. Not a sermon. Not a rule. Not even a name. But breath. The Spirit of God, poured into lungs, animating dust into dignity.

Every breath since then is a continuation of that first divine exhale.

And yet, in our modern chaos, we forget to breathe.

We race through life with shallow lungs and scattered minds. We hold our breath in traffic, in tension, in fear. We spend our days under-oxygenated, overstimulated, and utterly unaware that the very key to peace is already within us.

But mindfulness reminds us of the truth: **your breath is your anchor.**

It is how you return. To presence. To God. To yourself.

It is your compass in confusion, your ground in the storm.
It is not just air. It is Spirit.

The Breath as a Gateway to the Present

You don't have to be in a temple to experience the sacred.

You don't need a mountain or a monastery.

All you need… is breath.

Because breath is the doorway to now. And *now* is the only place God moves.

The past is a memory.
The future is a projection.
But the present—this breath—is where the holy lives.

When you pay attention to your breathing, something shifts. You become aware. You become grounded. You become available to the moment as it is—not as you wish it were, not as you fear it might be.

One conscious breath is a reset. A recalibration. A reminder: *I am here. God is here. And that is enough.*

You don't have to be fearless. Just breath-full.
You don't have to have it figured out. Just breathe into what is.

The breath brings your soul back online.
It anchors you when the winds of life try to carry you away.

Learning to Ride the Breath

When I first began practicing mindfulness, I didn't realize how often I was holding my breath.

I would clench during conflict. Tense up when I was overwhelmed. Shallow breathe when I felt insecure. My body was trying to stay alert— but it was doing so by shutting down my most vital connection to life.

One day, during a particularly anxious moment, I heard a whisper in my spirit say:

"Ride the breath."

It felt strange at first, but I closed my eyes and let the breath become like a wave—rising, cresting, falling, flowing. I followed it in and out, gently, like a boat riding the rhythm of the sea.

I imagined myself breathing in peace, and exhaling worry.
Breathing in grace, and exhaling shame.
Breathing in God, and exhaling everything that wasn't aligned with Him.

To "ride the breath" became more than a metaphor. It became my lifeline.

When your mind races, the breath grounds you.
When emotions overwhelm, the breath regulates you.
When everything feels chaotic, the breath returns you to your center—your Spirit-led center.

Breath is God's rhythm.
And when you ride it, you begin to remember your own divine tempo.

Breathwork and Nervous System Healing

Let's talk about the body. Because the breath is not just spiritual—it's physiological.

God created us with a nervous system that responds to threat and safety. When we feel danger—real or perceived—our body shifts into "fight or flight." Our heart rate increases. Muscles tense. Breathing becomes rapid and shallow.

This is helpful if you're facing a lion. But most of us are facing emails, finances, broken relationships, and chronic stress—not actual lions.

Unfortunately, our bodies don't know the difference. They still respond as if survival is at stake.

But here's the good news: **your breath can teach your body that it's safe.**

When you breathe slowly and deeply—especially into the belly—you activate the parasympathetic nervous system, also known as the "rest and restore" state. You literally signal to your brain: *It's okay. You're not in danger.*

This is why Scripture says:

> *"Let everything that has breath praise the Lord."* (Psalm 150:6)

Breath is not just a biological function—it's a form of worship and restoration.

Through breathwork, we partner with God's design for healing. We allow the body to recover. The mind to soften. The heart to open.

We return to our natural, Spirit-filled state: peace.

Guided Breathing Practices

Now that we understand the breath's sacred power, let's explore some simple, powerful practices that you can begin using today.

These are not mystical. They are not complicated. They are invitations to *come home to the present moment*, to your body, and to God.

1. 4-7-8 Breathing

This technique calms the nervous system and brings clarity.

How to practice:

- Inhale through your nose for 4 seconds
- Hold the breath for 7 seconds
- Exhale slowly through the mouth for 8 seconds
- Repeat for 4-6 cycles

Spiritual Intention: On the inhale, receive God's peace. On the exhale, release control.

2. Box Breathing (4-4-4-4)

Great for grounding and focus, often used by Navy SEALs and first responders.

How to practice:

- Inhale for 4 seconds
- Hold for 4 seconds
- Exhale for 4 seconds
- Hold again for 4 seconds
- Repeat for 4 rounds or more

Spiritual Intention: Visualize the breath drawing a square—stability, order, balance. You are supported by the divine on all sides.

3. Breath Awareness Meditation

This is a foundational practice. Simple, yet profound.

How to practice:

- Sit in a comfortable position
- Close your eyes and begin to notice the breath
- No need to change it—just observe
- When your mind wanders, gently return to the breath
- Practice for 5 to 10 minutes

Spiritual Intention: Each breath is a prayer. A meeting place. A return to God's presence.

Your Inhale Is Your Invitation Home

There's a moment at the beginning of every breath that feels like a doorway. A tiny threshold between unconsciousness and awareness.

If you listen closely, you'll hear it whisper: *Welcome back.*

Welcome back to your body.
Welcome back to the now.
Welcome back to the breath of God moving through you.

You don't need to run away to reset.
You don't need to have everything figured out.
You just need to breathe.

The world will still spin. The demands will still come. But you will be different. You will be anchored.

And that anchor—this breath—is the one thing no one can take from you.

It is your soul's rhythm.
It is God's Spirit within you.
It is your sacred ground.

A Breath and a Blessing

Before we close this chapter, take a deep, conscious breath.

Inhale: *God, fill me with your peace.*
Exhale: *I release all that is not mine to carry.*
Inhale: *I receive your Spirit, your wisdom, your calm.*
Exhale: *I return to the present, where You are.*

Breathe.
Trust.
Return.

Your breath is your anchor.
And with every breath, you are never alone.

CHAPTER 5:

THE BODY REMEMBERS

The body keeps score—
but it also holds wisdom.

> "Do you not know that your bodies are temples of the Holy Spirit, who is in you, whom you have received from God?"
> —1 Corinthians 6:19

For a long time, I lived almost entirely in my head.

I could think clearly. I could plan brilliantly. I could speak, perform, teach, achieve. But I could not *feel*. Or if I did, I didn't trust it. I'd learned early that my mind was a safer place than my body—because the body carries pain, and I wasn't ready to go there.

But the body is patient.

It waits for us. Quietly. Lovingly. Persistently.

Until one day, the ache in your chest won't go away. The knot in your stomach becomes unbearable. The exhaustion no longer lifts after sleep. And the whisper grows louder: *"There is something you need to feel."*

What I've learned on this journey is that the body doesn't just carry symptoms. It carries stories.
Not just biology—but biography.
Not just pain—but possibility.

And when we bring mindfulness into the body, we don't just find healing—we find God.

Because this body, this vessel, this sacred earth suit—is a holy temple. A living, breathing expression of Spirit. And it remembers everything we've lived through. Not to torment us, but to offer us the chance to be whole.

Somatic Mindfulness and Embodiment

Somatic means *of the body*. And mindfulness of the body is not about obsession with appearance or performance. It's about *presence*. Deep, compassionate, loving presence within the body that God gave you.

Most of us have learned to live *outside* of ourselves. We disassociate, disconnect, distract. We override our body's signals because they're inconvenient or confusing. We numb what we don't want to feel.

But the body never lies. It is always telling the truth.

When you tune in to the body—not through judgment, but through grace—you begin to notice where you are holding tension, fear, grief, or even joy.

You discover not just symptoms, but signals. Not just problems, but prayers.

Embodiment means living from the inside out.
It means not just being aware *of* your body—but *with* your body.
It means honoring it as the holy sanctuary it is.

When we drop out of the mind and into the body, we begin to heal the split between Spirit and self.

Noticing Tension, Signals, and Truth in the Body

Here's a truth we often overlook: the body speaks.

It speaks in language we may not have learned to hear. Tight shoulders. Racing heart. Shallow breath. Restlessness. Numbness. Or sometimes, pure calm.

Every physical sensation has something to teach us if we are willing to listen.

- A tight chest may be the body saying, *"I'm holding sadness."*
- A clenched jaw may be whispering, *"I'm not saying what I need to say."*
- A heavy stomach might be saying, *"I'm afraid of what's coming next."*

And just as pain speaks, so does peace.

- A soft belly might mean, *"I feel safe."*
- Open shoulders might signal, *"I'm free."*
- Steady breath might be God's voice saying, *"You are home."*

> The key is this: we do not observe to fix—we observe to *know*. To know ourselves. To know the truth. To know how to show up in grace.

When you start asking your body, *"What are you trying to tell me?"*— you open the door to revelation.

Movement and Stillness
The body needs both.

Sometimes healing comes in stillness—when we rest, when we breathe, when we allow ourselves to simply be.

But sometimes healing comes through movement—when we stretch, dance, walk, sway, or shake out the stagnant energy we've carried for far too long.

In my own practice, I began to notice that my prayers became more honest when I was moving.
That the Spirit would rise when I walked mindfully through nature.
That tears would come in a yoga pose, or laughter in spontaneous movement.

Movement is medicine. So is rest.
Stillness is sacred. So is embodiment.

Mindfulness allows you to discern what the moment calls for. Some days, you'll feel Spirit say, *"Be still."*
Other days, you'll hear, *"Move your body. Let it speak."*

Whether still or in motion, the body remains your spiritual ally—not your enemy. It carries the divine pulse of life. It is not a problem to be fixed. It is a prayer to be heard.

Body Scan Meditation and Mindful Walking
To deepen into this awareness, here are two simple yet profound practices that help you listen to your body and reconnect with its sacred intelligence.

1. Body Scan Meditation
This practice invites gentle, nonjudgmental awareness to different parts of the body.

How to practice:

- Sit or lie down in a comfortable position.
- Close your eyes and begin by bringing attention to your breath.
- Slowly move your attention from the crown of your head to your feet, noticing sensations, tension, or areas of ease.

- Simply observe. If you feel resistance, breathe love into that space.
- End by thanking your body for its wisdom and strength.

Spiritual Intention:
"God, show me where I need healing. Let me listen with compassion."

2. Mindful Walking
This practice reconnects movement with sacred awareness.

How to practice:

- Find a quiet space to walk slowly. Outdoors is ideal, but indoors works too.
- As you walk, pay attention to each step. Feel the contact of your foot with the ground.
- Let your arms swing naturally. Breathe in rhythm with your steps.
- With each step, say silently, *"I am here. God is here."*
- Let your mind settle into your feet, your breath, your body.

Spiritual Intention:
"Each step I take is with God. I walk in peace, I walk in love."

The Body as Holy Ground
There was a moment in prayer once when I asked God why I felt so far from Him, even while reading Scripture and serving others. I was spiritually hungry but emotionally numb.

The answer came not in a verse, but in a sensation. A warmth in my chest. A subtle vibration in my hands. A softening in my belly. And then, a whisper in my heart:

"I'm not just in your thoughts. I'm in your body too."

That was the beginning of a new understanding: that God does not just live in the mind or the heavens. God lives in *me*. In the breath. In the heart. In the sacred temple that is my body.

When I stretch, I worship.
When I rest, I restore.
When I dance, I delight.
When I listen, I heal.

You don't have to transcend the body to find God. You need only descend into it—with love.

Closing Reflection: Come Back to Your Body
Let's take a moment now.

Close your eyes.
Feel your body sitting, standing, lying—however you are.
Breathe into your belly.
Feel your heart.
Feel your feet.
Feel the presence of God, not just above you—but *within you*.

Say silently to your body:

"Thank you. I see you. I bless you. You are holy."

You may have abandoned your body. You may have rejected it.
But it has never abandoned you.

It has carried you through every storm.
Held your memories. Absorbed your pain.
And waited patiently—for this moment.

To be seen.
To be felt.
To be loved.

This is embodiment.
This is sacred awareness.
This is mindfulness in flesh.

Your body remembers—but it also releases.
Your body holds pain—but it also holds the presence of God.
Come home to your body.
It is not just where you live.
It is where the Holy lives in you.

CHAPTER 6:

EMOTIONAL ALCHEMY

Feel it,
to free it.

MINDFULNESS IS THE WAY • 61

> "The Lord is close to the brokenhearted
> and saves those who are crushed in spirit."
> —Psalm 34:18

There's a quiet moment in every healing journey where you stop running—not because you've found all the answers, but because you've grown tired of avoiding the truth of what you feel.

I remember mine clearly.

I had been carrying so much—grief, guilt, unspoken anger, shame. I thought I could think my way through it, analyze it, out-perform it. I even tried to "pray" it away, imagining that if I were just more faithful, more positive, more spiritual, I wouldn't feel so much.

But emotion isn't a flaw. It's a form of divine communication.

It wasn't until I finally allowed myself to *feel*—to weep, to tremble, to sit in silence with no answers—that I felt the presence of God begin to rise *within* the emotion. Not after it. Not around it. *Within it.*

That was the beginning of emotional alchemy.

Feeling Fully Without Judgment
We live in a world that has taught us to fear feelings.

Especially the "hard" ones—sadness, anger, anxiety, grief, loneliness. We're told to suck it up, move on, or fix it. And so we numb. We deny. We perform over the pain.

But mindfulness calls us back to a deeper truth:
You cannot heal what you refuse to feel.
And you cannot feel what you continue to judge.

God gave us emotions not to punish us, but to *guide* us. To alert us. To awaken us. To help us process, release, and return to alignment with His Spirit.

To feel mindfully is to let the emotion *move through you*—without attaching to it, without becoming it.

You are not your anger.
You are not your fear.
You are the one who can *hold space* for those emotions with compassion and grace.

Mindfulness invites you to be the sanctuary your emotions have always needed.

> "Come to me, all who are weary and burdened, and I will give you rest." (Matthew 11:28)

This isn't just about exhaustion from life. It's about the burden of *unfelt emotion*.

Mindfulness and Emotional Regulation

Let's be clear—feeling your emotions isn't about spiraling into them or being ruled by them. That's not presence—that's reactivity.

Mindfulness teaches us to feel *with awareness*, not to drown in the feeling, but to bring divine attention *to* the feeling.

This is emotional regulation:

- Not suppression.
- Not explosion.
- But sacred observation.

It's the ability to notice what arises, name it without shame, and stay connected to the breath, the body, and God's presence.

Through mindfulness, your nervous system learns:

"It is safe to feel this. I do not have to escape this. I can stay."

That *staying* is what transforms emotional chaos into spiritual clarity. That's what turns raw emotion into wisdom. That's the alchemy.

Turning Pain into Presence

Every wound has a voice. And every emotion is a messenger.

Grief might be asking you to honor what you've lost.
Anger might be showing you a boundary that's been crossed.
Fear might be inviting you into deeper trust.
Shame might be revealing where love needs to enter.

When you turn toward your pain, something sacred happens: you no longer become a prisoner to it. You become a witness. A healer. A participant in your own transformation.

Mindfulness teaches you how to hold pain with the love of Christ—not push it away, not drown in it, but *meet it* with presence.

When you bring the light of awareness into your pain, you create space for God to move *within* the pain—not just to remove it, but to *redeem it.*

That is the alchemy: pain becomes presence.
Wounds become wisdom.
Emotions become portals to grace.

The Sacred Pause

> One of the most powerful tools in mindfulness is what I call **The Sacred Pause.**

It's the moment between reaction and response. The breath before the words. The silence before the story. The stillness before the storm.

In that pause, something holy opens.

Instead of snapping, numbing, or overthinking, you stop. You return to the breath. You check in with the body. You ask the emotion, *"What are you here to show me?"*

You shift from automatic reaction to sacred presence.

This is where the Spirit meets you—not to erase your emotions, but to hold them with you.
To turn them from overwhelming floods into rivers of revelation.

The Sacred Pause is where reactivity ends and divine clarity begins.

Practices for Holding Emotion Mindfully
Let's ground these teachings in simple, spiritual practices to help you hold your emotions with grace.

1. RAIN Practice *(Tara Brach, adapted spiritually)*

R – **Recognize** the emotion that is present
A – **Allow** it to be there, without resistance
I – **Investigate** it with compassion: *What does it feel like in the body?*
N – **Nurture** the part of you that feels it: *How can I bring love here?*

Spiritual Integration: Invite God into the emotion as you practice. Imagine Christ sitting beside you, not judging, but holding your heart with sacred tenderness.

2. Name It to Tame It
Research shows that naming an emotion helps regulate the amygdala and brings the prefrontal cortex (wisdom brain) back online.

Simply say:

- "I'm feeling sadness."
- "This is fear."
- "Anger is here."

Then breathe. Stay. Bless yourself for noticing.

3. Hand on Heart Prayer
Place your hand gently over your heart. Breathe deeply.

Say aloud or silently:

"I am allowed to feel this. God, be near to me in this moment. Let your Spirit hold what I cannot yet hold on my own."

This physical and spiritual practice activates safety, compassion, and divine connection.

4. Emotional Journaling with God
Open a journal and write as if in conversation with God:

- *"God, today I feel..."*
- *"What is this emotion trying to tell me?"*
- *"Where do I need your peace right now?"*

Let the journaling become a prayer, a confession, and a return to grace.

The God Who Feels with Us
Never forget, we serve a God who feels.

Jesus wept.
Jesus grieved.
Jesus felt anger, compassion, exhaustion, love.

He was not above emotion—He was *fully present* in it.
That means you never walk alone in your emotional life.

You are not broken because you feel deeply.
You are not unspiritual because you struggle emotionally.

You are human. And in that humanity, divinity is not absent. It is alive.

Mindfulness helps you walk the way Jesus walked:
Present. Compassionate. Grounded in truth.
Moved by love, not by fear.

Closing Reflection: Emotions Are Teachers, Not Threats
Take a deep breath.
Close your eyes.
Notice what you're feeling right now—not to change it, but to *bless it.*

Say to yourself:

"Whatever I'm feeling is not too much for me. And it's certainly not too much for God. I am safe. I am loved. I am held."

Let this truth sink into your spirit:

You don't need to fight your emotions.
You don't need to be afraid of your heart.
You only need to stay. Breathe. Listen. Invite God in.

That is the path.
That is the healing.
That is emotional alchemy.

Your emotions are sacred messengers.
Your presence is the container.
God's Spirit is the transformer.
And together, they will lead you to peace.

CHAPTER 7:

THE SACRED
NOW

God meets you in
the moment.

> "Be still, and know that I am God."
> —Psalm 46:10

There is a sacred doorway that exists in every moment. A portal so powerful it can lead you out of anxiety, out of regret, out of illusion—and into truth.

It's not in the future you're striving toward.
It's not in the past you wish you could change.
It's *right here*. Right now.

This moment is the only place where life is truly lived, and it is the only place where God is fully present.

We often think that the sacred is somewhere far away—up in the heavens, behind the veil, in a church building or mountaintop. But Scripture reminds us again and again that God is near. Immanuel. *God with us.* Not just *back then*. Not just *one day*. But now.

The present moment is not just a blip on the timeline of your life. It is the altar.
It is the sanctuary.
It is the space where heaven touches earth.

Mindfulness helps us stop searching for God in the abstract and teaches us to find Him in the here and now.

The Theology of the Present Moment

God is not bound by time, but we are. And yet, in His grace, God meets us within time—in the only place we can truly encounter Him: the present.

The Bible doesn't say *"I was"* or *"I will be."* It says:

"I AM."

God's name is not a reference to the past or a promise of the future. It is an invitation into *presence*. Into divine immediacy.

Mindfulness is not about emptying the mind. It's about *entering into awareness*—awareness of breath, body, being, and above all, the presence of God who lives not in our fantasy or fear but in our *now*.

So many of us spend our lives living in yesterday's wounds or tomorrow's worries. We rehearse regrets. We project scenarios. We miss the miracle that is unfolding in this breath, this heartbeat, this sacred, ordinary second.

When we are not present, we miss God. Not because He has left us— but because we have left ourselves.

> "This is the day that the Lord has made; let us rejoice and be glad in it." (Psalm 118:24)

Not tomorrow. Not someday. But this day. This moment. This now.

God, Spirit, and the "I AM" in Mindfulness

As I deepened my own mindfulness practice, I began to hear the same truth echoed over and over in stillness:

"I am here."

Sometimes I heard it in a whisper while watching the sun rise. Sometimes I felt it while sitting in silence, tears streaming down my face. Sometimes it was in the breath itself—a pulse of sacred knowing.

God wasn't waiting for me to become perfect before He showed up.
He wasn't hiding in the future.
He was *right here*—in the middle of my fear, in the middle of my uncertainty, in the middle of my breath.

> The "I AM" isn't just a name. It's a divine presence. A holy reality. A love that is always *now*.

To practice mindfulness is to practice becoming available to the "I AM."

It's not a technique—it's a way of being. A way of awakening to what has always been true:

God is not far.
You are not alone.
The kingdom is not later.
It is *within you*. (Luke 17:21)

Aligning with Divine Timing
Let's be honest—most of us are either chasing the future or trying to outrun the past. We think peace will come when we get there, do that, fix this, change that. But that is the lie of hustle spirituality. The myth of someday salvation.

God is not in your *hustle*.
God is in your *here*.

Mindfulness teaches us to trust that we are where we need to be—even if it's uncomfortable, even if it's uncertain.

This doesn't mean we don't grow. But it means we don't have to leave the present to find peace. Because **transformation doesn't**

happen in the future. It begins the moment you become *present* to what is.

This is divine timing—not control, not anxiety, not force—but trust. Surrender. A sacred agreement to live in rhythm with the Spirit rather than in reaction to the world.

When you stop rushing the moment, the moment begins to reveal its purpose.

Awe, Grace, and Gratitude
One of the most beautiful fruits of mindfulness is awe.

When we slow down enough to *see*, everything becomes miraculous. The way light filters through the trees. The way your child's eyes crinkle when they laugh. The rhythm of your own breath. The fact that you are alive right now, on a spinning planet, sustained by unseen grace.

Awe is not an emotion. It's a spiritual posture.
It's what happens when you remember how holy the ordinary really is.

Gratitude naturally flows from awe. Not forced gratitude, but embodied gratitude—the kind that arises when you're actually present enough to notice what's right in front of you.

And in that noticing, you are changed.

You don't become more positive. You become more *awake*.
More in love with life. More attuned to the goodness of God.
Not because everything is perfect, but because *you are present to what is.*

> "Surely the Lord is in this place, and I was not aware of it."
> —Genesis 28:16

Mindfulness opens your awareness.
Gratitude opens your heart.
Awe opens your soul.

Practicing Presence: Returning to Now

Here are some soul-anchoring practices to help you return to the sacred now:

1. One Breath Meditation

You don't need 30 minutes. You need one moment.

Stop what you're doing.
Close your eyes.
Take one conscious breath.
Inhale: "I am."
Exhale: "Here."
Repeat if needed.

This is the reset button for your soul.

2. Five-Sense Check-In

Name:

- One thing you can see
- One thing you can hear
- One thing you can touch
- One thing you can smell
- One thing you can taste

This brings your awareness back to the *now* and anchors you in the body, where God meets you.

3. Sacred Sight Practice
Wherever you are, pause. Look around. Say silently:

"God, show me the sacred in this scene."

You might notice sunlight on the table. The curve of a loved one's face. A flicker of peace in your own chest.

You are training your eyes to see not just what is—but *Who is* present.

4. The Now Gratitude List
Write a short list each day of what you are grateful for *in this moment*. Not general. Not abstract. *Now.*

Examples:

- The way my coffee smells.
- The sound of my dog breathing nearby.
- The light coming through my blinds.
- The quiet I feel for the first time today.

Let these small gratitudes become your doorway to worship.

Closing Reflection: This Is Holy Ground
Right now, wherever you are—this moment is sacred.

You don't need to strive to get closer to God.
You only need to stop and see: *He is already here.*

Your breath is holy.
Your now is holy.
Your life is not waiting to begin—it's already happening.

Pause.
Breathe.
Be still.

And know—not just with your mind, but with your whole being:
God is here. I am here. And this is holy ground.

Welcome to the sacred now.
This is where you meet peace.
This is where you meet God.
This is where you meet yourself—finally, fully, faithfully.

CHAPTER 8:

MINDFUL RELATIONSHIPS

*Presence is the language
of love.*

> "Above all, love each other deeply, because love covers over a multitude of sins."
> —1 Peter 4:8

It is one thing to practice mindfulness in solitude.
It is another thing entirely to bring that presence into your relationships.

Solitude gives us space to breathe, to listen, to regulate.
But relationships—oh, relationships—they are where mindfulness is tested, embodied, and transformed into love.

Why?

Because relationships mirror us. They reveal our unhealed parts, our triggers, our projections, and our deepest needs. They are sacred ground, not because they are always easy, but because they offer us the opportunity to practice the greatest commandment in action: *to love one another.*

But you cannot love what you are not present to.
And you cannot be present to another if you are not first present to yourself.

Mindfulness, then, becomes the foundation for spiritual intimacy— not just with God, but with each other.

Listening Deeply, Speaking Truthfully

One of the most loving things you can ever do for someone is to truly listen—not to fix, not to advise, not to interrupt with your own experience—but to be fully, mindfully present to their voice, their heart, their pain.

We live in a world where most people are not listening. They are waiting to respond. Waiting to defend. Waiting to be heard.

But mindful listening is different. It is sacred. It is an act of humility and reverence.

> "Everyone should be quick to listen, slow to speak and slow to become angry." (James 1:19)

When you are truly present with someone:

- You hear beyond their words.
- You feel what they're not saying.
- You communicate: *You matter. I see you. I'm with you.*

And just as mindfulness teaches us to listen without judgment, it also teaches us to *speak without harm*. To speak with truth, but also with tenderness. With clarity, but also with care.

Speaking truthfully doesn't mean unloading emotion without wisdom. It means choosing words that align with your soul, honor the Spirit, and leave space for grace.

"Let your conversation be always full of grace, seasoned with salt." —Colossians 4:6

Mindfulness slows you down enough to *feel what's true*, so your words can be both honest and healing.

Compassion Without Codependence
There is a difference between compassion and emotional enmeshment.

Mindfulness allows you to hold space for another person without losing yourself in their experience.

This is especially important in close relationships—spouses, partners, children, parents, deep friendships—where emotions can easily become blurred and boundaries easily crossed.

Compassion says, *"I see your pain and I care."*
Codependence says, *"Your pain is my responsibility, and I cannot rest until you're okay."*

One is rooted in presence.
The other in fear.

When you are mindful, you can notice when you are absorbing emotions that aren't yours, over-functioning, rescuing, or reacting out of guilt instead of grounded love.

Mindfulness helps you stay in your body, in your center, in your Spirit-led truth.

You can still empathize—but from a place of peace. You can still help—but from a place of clarity. You can still love—but without abandoning yourself.

This is holy compassion. This is Christlike presence.

Conflict Resolution Through Presence
Even the most loving relationships experience conflict. But what determines the health of a relationship is not the absence of disagreement—it's the presence of *awareness* during disagreement.

Mindfulness transforms conflict.

Instead of reacting from old wounds, you pause.
Instead of yelling, you breathe.
Instead of shutting down, you stay present to your body, your breath, your truth.

This sacred pause creates room for:

- Slower speech
- Deeper listening
- Less blame
- More understanding
- Genuine resolution

Mindfulness invites us to become curious instead of critical. To say, *"What am I feeling?"* before *"What did you do wrong?"* It teaches us to seek understanding before victory. It reminds us that love is not proven in being right—but in staying connected even when things get hard.

> "Let us pursue what makes for peace and for mutual upbuilding." —Romans 14:19

Conflict becomes not a battle to win but a mirror to grow.

Relational Mindfulness Practices
Here are a few practices that will help you bring mindfulness into your relationships and live in divine connection with others:

1. The 3-Breath Presence Check-In (Before Hard Conversations)
Before speaking, pause for three conscious breaths.

- Inhale: *"I am here."*
- Inhale: *"This person is not my enemy."*
- Inhale: *"God, help me speak in love."*

This anchors your body and Spirit before engaging.

2. Eye Gazing (Soul-to-Soul Presence)
Sit across from a loved one. No words. Just eye contact for 1–2 minutes.

Breathe. Notice. Stay open.

Let this be a silent prayer: *"I see you. I honor the image of God in you."*

3. Mindful Listening Exercise
Take 5–10 minutes where one person speaks while the other only listens—no advice, no interruptions. Then switch.

Finish with this question: *"What did you hear me say—not just in words, but in feeling?"*

This deepens understanding and dissolves assumptions.

4. Loving-Kindness Prayer (Metta Prayer)
Bring to mind someone you love. Then someone neutral. Then someone difficult.

Silently pray:

"May you be safe.
May you be well.
May you be at peace.
May you know the love of God."

This practice stretches your heart and grows your compassion muscle.

Relationships as Reflections of God

Our relationships are not separate from our spiritual path. They *are* the path.

We learn how to love not just in solitude, but in the sacred mess of daily life—with those who challenge us, support us, reflect us, and sometimes wound us.

And every relationship, no matter how brief or broken, is an invitation:

- To practice presence.
- To extend compassion.
- To see God in the face of the other.

When you are mindful in your relationships, you begin to witness the Divine not only *in* the other person—but *through* the relationship itself.

A spouse becomes a mirror.
A child becomes a teacher.
A stranger becomes a reminder of shared humanity.
A difficult person becomes a catalyst for your growth in grace.

Mindfulness turns everyday encounters into holy communion.

Closing Reflection: Let Love Be Present

Take a breath.

Bring to mind someone close to you—maybe someone you love dearly, or someone with whom you've recently had tension.

Place your hand over your heart and breathe in love.
On the exhale, release control.
On the next inhale, invite God's Spirit to move in your relationship.

Say silently:

"God, help me show up with presence.
Help me listen without judgment.
Help me love without fear.
Let Your peace move through me."

Let love become your practice.
Let presence become your posture.
Let your relationships become your prayer.

This is mindful love.
This is mindful relationship.
This is The Way.

Love is not a feeling.
It is presence.
It is attention.
It is the choice to be here—fully, honestly, humbly, and sacredly.

CHAPTER 9:

THE NOISE
DETOX

*Silence is not empty—it's
full of answers.*

> "In repentance and rest is your salvation,
> in quietness and trust is your strength."
> —Isaiah 30:15

It's loud out there.

Even when no one is speaking, the world hums with constant motion. Our phones buzz. Alerts chime. Ads flash. Background music fills every room. Even in solitude, our inner voice rarely stops talking.

Noise has become our default. We wear it like armor. We use it to fill the space, to distract from the ache, to avoid the stillness we're secretly afraid of.

But here's the sacred truth: **you cannot hear the voice of God if your life is too loud.**
And more often than not, the soul doesn't need more advice—it needs more *silence*.

Social Media, Overstimulation, and Digital Mindfulness
Let's talk about screens.

Most of us spend more time each day in front of a screen than we do in face-to-face connection, embodied awareness, or prayerful reflection. Our attention is constantly pulled toward headlines, hashtags, and highlight reels.

We scroll when we're bored.
We scroll when we're lonely.
We scroll to avoid the discomfort of our own thoughts.

And it's not just social media. It's the never-ending notifications, emails, podcasts, news cycles. The digital world trains our brain to expect constant input and instant stimulation.

But this comes at a cost.

- We lose our capacity for stillness.
- We damage our ability to focus.
- We forget how to simply *be* without consuming something.

Even more dangerously, we begin to forget the sound of our own soul—and the gentle whisper of God's voice within us.

Digital mindfulness doesn't mean going off the grid. It means *taking back your attention* and using technology as a tool, not a tyrant.

Creating Sacred Space for Silence

There is a holiness in quiet that our world has forgotten. But God has not.

> "The Lord is in his holy temple; let all the earth keep silence before him." —Habakkuk 2:20

Silence is not the absence of sound—it is the *presence of presence.* A stillness that holds space for what's real. A sanctuary that opens within when the outer world fades.

When you intentionally create silence—whether for five minutes or an entire day—you are making room for the sacred.

Your soul knows what to do in silence.
It breathes. It listens. It remembers.

Some of the most healing moments of my life have come not through words, but through stillness.
Not through figuring it out, but through *laying it down*.

You don't need a mountaintop or monastery. You can create sacred space wherever you are:

- A quiet corner in your home
- A bench in a park
- A pause in the car before going inside
- A minute of breath between meetings

Silence is not a luxury. It's a lifeline.

Fasting from Distraction

Just as we fast from food to cleanse the body, we can fast from noise to clear the spirit.

A noise fast may look like:

- A day without music or podcasts
- A week off social media
- A few hours of screen-free time each evening
- A silent morning ritual
- A digital Sabbath once a week

At first, it may feel uncomfortable—even agitating. That's okay. That discomfort is your nervous system recalibrating. Your mind detoxing. Your soul stretching into the space it's long been denied.

In the beginning, silence may expose what you've been avoiding. But stay with it. Because just beyond that initial unease is a peace the world cannot give.

> "Jesus often withdrew to lonely places and prayed." (Luke 5:16)

If Jesus needed solitude, so do we.

This isn't isolation—it's *intimacy* with God.

Practicing Presence in a Noisy World

We can't always control our environment. But we can learn to carry presence into any environment.

Even in the middle of chaos, you can cultivate a quiet mind. A grounded body. A still soul.

Here are some practices for bringing a mindful presence into everyday noise:

1. One-Minute Sound Awareness Meditation

Close your eyes.
Listen to the sounds around you without labeling them good or bad.
Just *notice*.
Let each sound 'come and go' like waves.
Anchor your awareness in the *space* between the sounds.

Spiritual Intention:

"I am not the noise. I am the awareness that hears it. God is in this space."

2. Digital Sabbath Practice

Pick one day a week or even just a few hours to turn off all devices.
No scrolling. No streaming. No email.

Use that time for:

- Reading Scripture
- Journaling
- Resting
- Taking a mindful walk
- Simply sitting in silence

Let your attention return to what matters most.

3. The Sacred Pause Before Response
Before answering a text, replying to an email, or reacting to a post—pause.
Take one conscious breath.
Ask: *"Am I responding from presence or from pressure?"*

Let your response reflect your intention, not your impulse.

4. Creating a Quiet Corner
Designate a small area in your home as your sacred space.
It doesn't have to be elaborate. A candle. A cushion. A Bible or journal.
Let this be your daily meeting place with God. A visual reminder that silence is sacred.

The Blessing of Quiet
Silence is not empty space—it is *pregnant* with the Spirit.

When we choose silence, we choose surrender.
We let go of the need to always know, always talk, always prove.
We become available—not just to ourselves, but to the presence of God.

"In quietness and trust is your strength."
Not in hustle. Not in noise. Not in endless information.

True strength is spiritual stillness.

In a world obsessed with louder, faster, more—we are called to live quieter, deeper, slower. Not because we are weak—but because we have remembered where strength really comes from.

From the whisper.
From the stillness.
From the silence where God speaks.

Closing Reflection: Let Stillness Speak
Take a deep breath.
Turn off the noise—just for a moment.
Place your hand on your heart.
Feel the quiet between the beats.
That's the doorway. The sacred now.

Say silently:

"God, meet me in the silence.
Still my mind.
Quiet my soul.
Let Your presence rise in this holy hush."

Let this be your prayer:

Not more. Not louder. Not faster.
But *here*.
But *quiet*.
But *holy*.

You do not need to fear silence.
It is not the absence of life.
It is the beginning of listening.
And the voice you're waiting for?
It speaks in the quiet.
It sounds like peace.
It sounds like home.
It sounds like God.

CHAPTER 10

PURPOSE, FLOW, AND THE PRESENT PATH

*You are most powerful
when you are present.*

> "For we are God's masterpiece. He has created us anew in Christ Jesus, so we can do the good things he planned for us long ago."
> —Ephesians 2:10

There's a question that quietly pulses in every human heart:

Why am I here?

It lives under our ambitions, our fears, our plans. It visits us in the night when the applause fades and the inbox is empty. It lingers in the pause between seasons, in the ache for more, in the longing to matter.

This question is not a flaw. It's a compass.

Because we were never created to simply exist—we were created to *live with purpose*.

But here's what many of us have misunderstood:
Purpose is not something you chase.
It's something you *align with*.

You don't need to run toward it—it's already within you.
What you need is presence.
Clarity.
Stillness.

Mindfulness doesn't just help you find your purpose.
It *teaches* you how to *live it*.

Living Mindfully into Your Purpose

There is a way to live that is not driven by ego or exhaustion, but by alignment.

It's not about "doing big things" or "leaving a legacy" for the sake of validation.
It's about waking up to the truth that your very existence—your breath, your kindness, your attention—is part of something eternal.

You are not a mistake.
You were handcrafted by God, infused with divine gifts, and planted in this time and place for reasons deeper than your resume can express.

But purpose is not a destination.
It's a way of being.
It's not found in the next opportunity—it's *revealed through presence.*

When you are mindful—fully attuned to the moment—you begin to see the fingerprints of purpose everywhere:

- In how you listen to someone who's hurting
- In the way you create, serve, teach, nurture, or lead
- In the small, unseen moments of faithfulness that align you with the Spirit

Purpose is not only in *what* you do. It's in *how* you do it.
Mindfully. Intentionally. With God.

Flow States and Divine Alignment

There is a state of being that every soul longs for—a rhythm where time fades, effort feels effortless, and creativity flows like a river.

Psychologists call it *flow.*
Athletes call it *the zone.*
Scripture might call it *abiding.*
"Abide in me, and I in you." (John 15:4)

To live in flow is to be so attuned to your purpose, your gifts, and the present moment that everything seems to *move through you* rather than *from you*.

This is not about ease without effort—but about *energy without resistance*.

Mindfulness cultivates the conditions for flow:

- Stillness in the mind
- Openness in the heart
- Presence in the body
- Surrender in the spirit

When you are mindful, you stop overthinking and start allowing. You stop performing and start *participating* in what God is already doing.

You align not just with your calling—but with your Creator.

Flow is not a superpower.
It is the fruit of presence, purpose, and Spirit working in harmony.

Replacing Hustle with Harmony
We live in a world that worships the hustle.

Hustle culture says:

- Do more.
- Prove yourself.
- Never stop.
- Rest is weakness.
- Your worth is in your productivity.

But the soul knows better.

> The soul longs for harmony, not hype.
> For flow, not frenzy.
> For peace, not pressure.

Mindfulness invites us to trade:

- *Control for curiosity*
- *Perfectionism for presence*
- *Overwhelm for surrender*

Jesus Himself modeled a life of rhythm—not rush. He worked, He taught, He healed. But He also withdrew, rested, prayed, and stayed connected to the Father.

If the Son of God didn't hustle, why should we?

Living mindfully into your purpose doesn't mean doing less.
It means doing what matters *from a grounded, grace-filled place.*

It means asking:

"Is this aligned with who God made me to be?"
"Is this how I want to show up in the world?"
"Is this from love... or from fear?"

Harmony isn't passive—it's powerful.
And it begins with presence.

Creating a Mindful Daily Rhythm

Your purpose is not found in occasional breakthroughs. It's revealed through *daily intention.*

The way you live each day is the way you live your life.
And mindfulness is the thread that weaves sacred presence through every moment.

Here are a few practices to help you live your purpose *on purpose*:

1. Morning Alignment Ritual

Before picking up your phone or to-do list, begin your day in stillness.

- Breathe deeply.
- Place your hand on your heart.
- Say: *"God, align me with Your will today. Let me live from peace, not pressure."*
- Ask: *"What do I want to embody today?"*

Let your day flow from this alignment.

2. Purposeful Pause Check-Ins

Set reminders throughout your day to pause and ask:

"Am I present?"
"Is what I'm doing aligned with love?"
"How is my body feeling in this moment?"

This practice helps you course-correct in real time and return to intention.

3. Flow Journal Reflection (Evening)

At the end of the day, reflect:

- When did I feel most alive or connected today?
- What moments felt natural, joyful, or Spirit-led?
- What drained me or felt forced?

Look for patterns. Let them guide your next day's focus.

4. Weekly Purpose Reset

Once a week, create space to reconnect with the bigger picture.

- Reflect on your gifts, desires, and dreams.
- Ask God: *"Where are You leading me?"*
- List one way you can serve or show up more fully in alignment this week.

Let purpose become a lived rhythm, not a lofty idea.

Closing Reflection: Walk the Present Path

You don't need to have it all figured out.

You don't need a ten-year plan.
You don't need everyone's approval.
You just need the next right step—taken in love, guided by presence, aligned with Spirit.

This is the path.

Your purpose is not a mountaintop—it's a way of walking.
One mindful step. One sacred yes. One breath of trust at a time.

So take a breath.

Right now.

Inhale: *"God, I trust Your timing."*
Exhale: *"I surrender my striving."*
Inhale: *"I walk in purpose."*
Exhale: *"I walk in peace."*

The path is not out there.
It is right beneath your feet.
Your presence is your power.
Your purpose is already unfolding.
Let mindfulness lead the way.

CHAPTER 11:

MINDFULNESS IN SUFFERING

Even in darkness,
the Way remains.

> "Even though I walk through the valley of the shadow of death,
> I will fear no evil, for You are with me."
> —Psalm 23:4

There are moments when life brings us to our knees.

Moments when the pain is so heavy that no words can reach it. Moments when our spiritual practices, no matter how sincere, seem too small to carry the weight of what we're feeling.

Grief. Loss. Trauma. Illness. Depression. Disappointment.

We know what it's like to sit in the ashes of something we thought would never fall apart. We've wept prayers that had no eloquence—just breath, or silence, or aching groans that words could never translate.

And in those moments, we often ask:

"Where is God in this?"

The answer, though not always loud, is always present:

Here. With you. In it.

Not bypassing it.
Not rushing it.
Not promising to remove every ounce of pain—but *promising never to leave you in it alone.*

Suffering doesn't mean God has gone silent.
It means He's whispering in a different language—one only the stillness of mindfulness and the softness of faith can truly hear.

When Presence Meets Pain

Mindfulness does not eliminate suffering.
But it *changes our relationship to it*.

It teaches us how to meet pain—not with fear or resistance—but with the tender, grounded awareness that says, *"This too belongs. This too is seen."*

It allows us to stay with our sorrow, without being consumed by it.
To breathe in the darkness, without losing the light.
To witness what hurts, without becoming the hurt itself.

In mindfulness, we don't bypass pain—we *bear witness to it*.

Like Mary at the foot of the cross, we stay present even in the agony.
Not because it's easy. But because *love doesn't look away*.

And in doing so, we begin to realize:

Suffering, when held in mindful presence, can become a holy space.
A crucible of transformation.
A garden where something new might one day grow—not despite the pain, but because of it.

Holding Grief, Trauma, and Uncertainty

There are seasons in life when clarity disappears.

The plans fall apart. The diagnosis arrives. The phone call comes. The rug gets pulled out from under your feet.

In those seasons, the soul doesn't need quick answers. It needs *companionship.*

Mindfulness becomes that companion.

It says:

"You don't have to fix this right now."
"You don't have to rush past your grief."
"You are allowed to feel the fullness of this moment."

Grief is not something to "get over."
It is a process to walk through.
Mindfully. Tenderly. Prayerfully.

Trauma, too, requires this sacred gentleness. It must be felt in safe doses. Held in compassion. Named without shame.

Uncertainty invites the same kind of presence—an open-handed faith that doesn't demand control, but chooses trust one breath at a time.

Mindfulness offers us a refuge within the storm.

Not a way to escape—but a way to *endure with grace.*

Surrender as Healing
There comes a point in suffering where striving simply doesn't work.

The answers don't come. The healing isn't instant. The weight is still there.

And in that holy breaking point, mindfulness teaches us how to *surrender*.

Not in defeat—but in **divine trust.**

To surrender is to lay your pain at the feet of God.
To stop asking *why* and begin asking *how*:

"How do I hold this moment with grace?"
"How do I stay present when everything in me wants to run?"
"How do I let go without losing myself?"

Surrender is not passive. It's the bravest kind of openness.
It says, *"I can't control this, but I can choose how I respond to it."*

And in that response, healing begins—not always of the body or the circumstance, but of the soul.

> "Cast all your anxiety on Him, because He cares for you."
> —1 Peter 5:7

Even when you don't feel strong, surrender lets God be strong for you.

The Role of Faith and Resilience

Mindfulness teaches us presence.
Faith teaches us perseverance.
Together, they create a soul that can endure the fire—and come out refined.

You can be mindful *and* angry.
You can be mindful *and* heartbroken.
You can be mindful *and* full of faith that God is still working in the silence.

Resilience isn't about denying pain—it's about choosing not to be defined by it.

When you suffer mindfully, you don't numb or avoid.
You breathe.

You pray.
You show up for the next moment.

And slowly, something sacred starts to rise: *the unbreakable part of you.*
The part the storm could not touch.
The part made in the image of a suffering Savior who knows what it means to bleed and to rise.

> Mindfulness gives you tools.
> Faith gives you hope.
> Together, they help you keep walking—one sacred step at a time.

Practices for Being Present in Suffering
Here are a few gentle tools for walking through pain with mindfulness and Spirit:

1. Compassionate Presence Prayer
Place your hand over your heart.
Take three deep, slow breaths.
Say aloud or silently:

"God, I am here.
This is hard.
But I do not walk through this alone.
Hold me in your presence.
Let your Spirit sit with me in this pain."

Repeat as needed.

2. The "Stay" Practice

When a painful emotion arises:

- Pause.
- Name it gently: *"This is grief."*
- Feel where it lives in your body.
- Place your breath there like a warm hand.
- Stay. Just for a moment. And breathe.

Staying is how the pain begins to transform.

3. Suffering Journal Reflection

Write in conversation with God:

- "This is what I'm carrying..."
- "This is what I don't understand..."
- "God, if you are here in this, show me where..."

Let the pages become your altar. Let honesty become your prayer.

4. The Grounding Walk

Take a slow, silent walk.
With each step, repeat:

"I am still here.
God is still here.
This pain is not the end of the story."

Let nature, movement, and breath become a sanctuary.

Closing Reflection: The Presence That Carries You

If you are walking through pain right now, let this be your reminder:

You do not have to do it perfectly.
You do not have to heal all at once.
You do not have to be strong every second.

You only need to *stay present*.
One breath.
One moment.
One whisper of prayer at a time.

> "Come to Me, all who are weary and burdened, and I will give you rest." (Matthew 11:28)

Not more pressure.
Not more answers.
Rest.

Let your suffering become a sanctuary.
Let your breath become your prayer.
Let your presence become your path.

You are not alone.
You never have been.
You never will be.

God is with you.
Right here.
Right now.
Even in this.

Even in the valley, there is a Way.
Even in the suffering, there is a light.
And even in your pain, there is Presence.

CHAPTER 12:

BECOMING
THE WAY

Your life becomes
your message.

MINDFULNESS IS THE WAY • 121

> "Let your light so shine before men,
> that they may see your good works and glorify your Father
> in heaven."
> —Matthew 5:16

We began this journey with a question:
"What if presence is the path?"

Now, having walked through breath, body, emotion, silence, suffering, and soul, the answer reveals itself:

It is.

Mindfulness is not merely a practice. It is not just meditation or breathing or noticing your thoughts.
It is a way of being. A way of seeing. A way of *living in alignment with the Divine Presence* that has always been with you—and within you.
And the final invitation of this journey is this:

Become the Way.

Let mindfulness move from your journal into your joy.
From your cushion into your conversation.
From your solitude into your service.

Let your life be the living evidence of what it means to walk in awareness, compassion, and Spirit-filled love.

Because the world doesn't need more information.
It needs more *embodied transformation*.
And that begins with you.

Living as a Mindful Presence in the World
Imagine a world where your presence changes the atmosphere.

Not because you're louder, faster, or more accomplished—but because you are deeply *here.*
Attuned. Centered. Awake.

That's the power of mindful presence.

It allows you to:

- Speak with clarity instead of defensiveness.
- Listen with compassion instead of judgment.
- Move with intention instead of impulse.
- Serve with joy instead of burnout.
- Rest with permission instead of guilt.

You become the person who slows down enough to see others. To breathe with them. To sit with them. To love them.

And in doing so, you reflect the image of Christ—not through performance, but through *presence.*

> "The Word became flesh and made His dwelling among us."
> (John 1:14)

Mindfulness helps you do the same.

You embody truth.
You inhabit love.
You become the dwelling place of peace.

Mindfulness as a Lifestyle and Legacy

The greatest gift you can give this world is *your transformed self.*

Not your perfect self.
Not your polished self.
Your **present** self.

When mindfulness becomes your way of life, it naturally begins to ripple outward—into your relationships, your work, your parenting, your leadership, your ministry.

You shift from chasing legacy to *living it.*

Your children will remember how calm you were, not how busy.
Your coworkers will remember your empathy, not your urgency.
Your friends will remember your listening, not your productivity.

And long after you're gone, the way you walked through the world—with grace, with presence, with Spirit—will linger like incense in the rooms you once occupied.

This is legacy: the memory of your presence becoming someone else's permission to slow down and come home to themselves.

Daily Rituals, Reminders, and Reflection

How do we sustain this? How do we live as the Way, not just in moments, but in the rhythm of our lives?

We create rituals—not rigid routines, but soul-nourishing practices that reconnect us to the sacred now.

Here are some daily anchors to help you embody mindfulness as a lifestyle:

1. The Morning Recommitment
Before the day pulls you outward, begin by going inward.

- Sit in stillness.
- Breathe deeply.
- Whisper: *"God, let me walk in presence today. Let me live from love, not fear."*
- Read a verse. Set an intention. Align your soul.

2. The Midday Reset
Take five minutes to pause.

- Step away from screens.
- Place your hand on your heart.
- Ask: *"Am I present?"*
- Breathe. Re-center. Recommit.

3. The Evening Integration
Close the day mindfully.

- Light a candle.
- Reflect: *"Where was I most present today? Where did I drift?"*
- Give thanks. Offer grace. Let go.

You're not aiming for perfection. You're cultivating *awareness.*

30-Day Mindfulness Roadmap

A Daily Journey into Presence, Peace, and Divine Alignment

> *"In returning and rest you shall be saved; in quietness and trust shall be your strength."* —Isaiah 30:15

Each day for the next 30 days, you are invited to walk the sacred path of mindful living by anchoring in four simple practices:

The Daily Rhythm

1. 5 Minutes of Breath Awareness
   Practice being fully present with each inhale and exhale. Let the breath bring you home to the moment.
   → *"The breath of the Almighty gives me life."* —Job 33:4
2. One Act of Mindful Listening
   Whether with God, a loved one, or your own heart—listen without fixing, judging, or rushing.
   → *"Everyone should be quick to listen, slow to speak..."* —James 1:19
3. A Gratitude for This Present Moment
   Acknowledge one thing—however small—that anchors you in the beauty of now. Let it become a quiet offering.
   → *"This is the day the Lord has made; we will rejoice and be glad in it."* —Psalm 118:24
4. A Short Prayer of Alignment
   Pray to be aligned with God's will and presence. Ask for guidance, stillness, and clarity.
   → *"Speak, Lord, for your servant is listening."* —1 Samuel 3:10

Weekly Themes for Reflection
To add depth and intention, each week includes a spiritual theme for contemplation and journaling.

Week 1: Awareness
Begin noticing your thoughts, breath, emotions, and surroundings. Let mindfulness meet the mundane.

Prompt: Where in my day am I most disconnected—and how can I return?

Week 2: Stillness

Cultivate internal quiet. Let go of the need to fill every silence. Let God speak in the pause.

Prompt: What am I filling my silence with, and what is God inviting me to hear instead?

Week 3: Presence

Let go of past and future stories. Practice being fully here, fully now—with full trust in divine timing.

Prompt: In what ways have I overlooked the sacredness of this moment?

Week 4: Alignment

Align your heart with your purpose. Let your spirit flow with God's rhythm, not the world's rush.

Prompt: Where in my life am I out of sync with God—and what needs to shift?

Reflection & Realignment (Day 30)

Spend today reviewing your journey:

- What changed in your inner world?
- How did daily presence impact your peace?
- What sacred rhythms do you want to continue?

> *"You will keep in perfect peace those whose minds are steadfast, because they trust in you."* —Isaiah 26:3

The Way Is Within You

Let this final truth echo through your spirit:

You don't need to become someone else.
You don't need to reach another milestone before you're allowed to feel peace.
You don't need to wait for a perfect season to walk in your calling.

You are already enough.
You are already held.
You are already the Way—because the Way lives in you.

> "I am the Way, the Truth, and the Life." —John 14:6

Jesus is not just a path to follow.
He is a presence to embody.
And mindfulness opens you to His indwelling Spirit, moment by moment, breath by breath.

This book may be ending—but your journey is not.

Every moment is a new beginning.
Every breath is a fresh return.
Every step is a sacred opportunity to live awake, aligned, and anchored in God.

So, go.

Live slowly.
Love deeply.
Listen closely.
And let the presence of the Holy within you become a healing presence in the world around you.

You are the witness.
You are the way.
You are the walking sanctuary.

This is *Mindfulness is The Way*.
And now, you are becoming... *The Way*.

EPILOGUE:

THE JOURNEY CONTINUES

This is not the end.
It is a new beginning.

You have walked with your breath.
You have listened to your body.
You have sat with your emotions, your fears, your longing.
You have heard the whisper of the sacred in the silence between thoughts.

And now, something in you has shifted. Not because you've arrived somewhere new—but because you've awakened to where you've always been.

This journey was never about escape.
It was about *return.*
A return to the now.
A return to God.
A return to your truest self.

So let this be your blessing:

Let every breath remind you—you are alive.
Let every moment teach you—you are not alone.
Let every now become your altar—where the Divine meets you in the ordinary.

You will forget. That's human.
But now you know how to return.
To the breath. To the body. To the presence of God within and around you.

Mindfulness is not the end of the journey.
It is the compass for the rest of your life.

It won't always be easy. But it will always be sacred.

Because *this*—this breath, this step, this silence, this joy, this sorrow—*this* is the Way.

And now, it is yours to live.

Go gently.
Go mindfully.
Go wholly... **be The Way.**

www.ingramcontent.com/pod-product-compliance
Lightning Source LLC
Chambersburg PA
CBHW060327050426
42449CB00011B/2687